JAN 1 2 2021

DISCOVERIES AROUND THE WORLD

GREAT MINDS AND FINDS IN
SOUTH AMERICA

Robin Koontz

ROurke
Educational Media

A Division of
Carson
Dellosa
Education

Bridges

Before Reading: *Building Background Knowledge and Vocabulary*

Building background knowledge can help children process new information and build upon what they already know. Before reading a book, it is important to tap into what children already know about the topic. This will help them develop their vocabulary and increase their reading comprehension.

Questions and Activities to Build Background Knowledge:

1. Look at the front cover of the book and read the title. What do you think this book will be about?
2. What do you already know about this topic?
3. Take a book walk and skim the pages. Look at the table of contents, photographs, captions, and bold words. Did these text features give you any information or predictions about what you will read in this book?

Vocabulary: *Vocabulary Is Key to Reading Comprehension*

Use the following directions to prompt a conversation about each word.

- Read the vocabulary words.
- What comes to mind when you see each word?
- What do you think each word means?

Vocabulary Words:

- agriculture
- aqueducts
- astronomy
- canopy
- conservation
- extinction
- Indigenous
- irrigation
- observatories
- terraces

During Reading: *Reading for Meaning and Understanding*

To achieve deep comprehension of a book, children are encouraged to use close reading strategies. During reading, it is important to have children stop and make connections. These connections result in deeper analysis and understanding of a book.

 Close Reading a Text

During reading, have children stop and talk about the following:

- Any confusing parts
- Any unknown words
- Text to text, text to self, text to world connections
- The main idea in each chapter or heading

Encourage children to use context clues to determine the meaning of any unknown words. These strategies will help children learn to analyze the text more thoroughly as they read.

When you are finished reading this book, turn to the next-to-last page for **Text-Dependent Questions** and an **Extension Activity**.

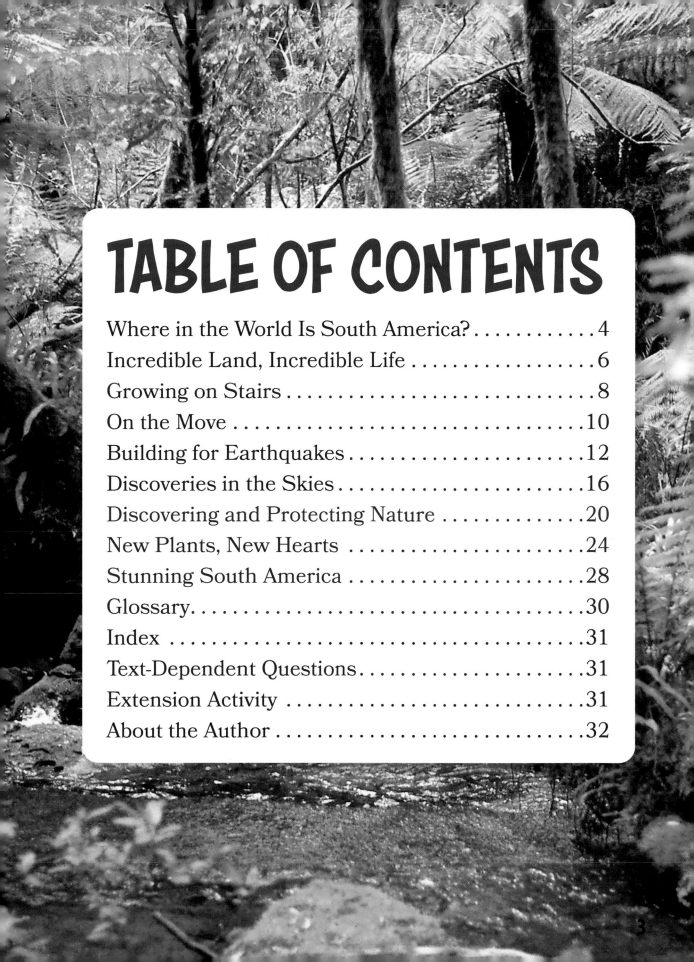

TABLE OF CONTENTS

Where in the World Is South America? 4

Incredible Land, Incredible Life 6

Growing on Stairs 8

On the Move 10

Building for Earthquakes 12

Discoveries in the Skies 16

Discovering and Protecting Nature 20

New Plants, New Hearts 24

Stunning South America 28

Glossary. 30

Index 31

Text-Dependent Questions. 31

Extension Activity 31

About the Author 32

WHERE IN THE WORLD IS SOUTH AMERICA?

South America is the fourth largest continent. It contains 12 countries and is surrounded by the Pacific and Atlantic oceans as well as the Caribbean Sea. South America is connected to North America by a strip of land only about 50 miles (82 kilometers) wide at its most narrow point.

SOUTH
AMERICA

Mount Aconcagua

The land connecting South and North America, shown here in a photo taken high in the air, is called the Isthmus of Panama.

South America by the Numbers

Population: >423 million

Size: >6.89 million square miles or >17.8 million square kilometers

Highest Point: Aconcagua, >22,841 feet or 6,962 meters

INCREDIBLE LAND, INCREDIBLE LIFE

South America is full of amazing sights. The Atacama Desert in the country of Chile is one of the driest deserts on Earth. The Andes mountains make up one of the world's longest mountain ranges. In each of these different places are plants and animals unlike anyplace else.

The Andes mountain range has different environments, including grasslands and volcanoes.

The Atacama Desert has an average rainfall of 0.6 inches (about 15 mm) a year.

South America has been home to many different forms of life throughout history, including over 200 kinds of dinosaurs. The scientist Pablo Gallina and his team discovered a new dinosaur in the country of Argentina, the *Bajadasaurus*.

In 2017, scientist Tom Dillehay and his team discovered signs of humans from about 15,000 years ago. A huge dirt mound in the country of Peru held stone tools, bones, and other evidence of some of the earliest Americans ever found.

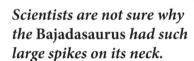

Scientists are not sure why the Bajadasaurus *had such large spikes on its neck.*

Recovered History

The oldest human fossil found in South America was discovered in the country of Brazil. Archaeologist Annette Laming-Emperaire discovered the woman, named "Luzia," in a cave. Scientists made a model of what she might have looked like, shown here.

GROWING ON STAIRS

Early South American people developed methods for **agriculture** that gave them better and more food. The Chimú were one of the earliest cultures in South America. They discovered ways to set up **irrigation** systems including farms, **aqueducts**, fountains, and canals. Many of their systems are still being used today.

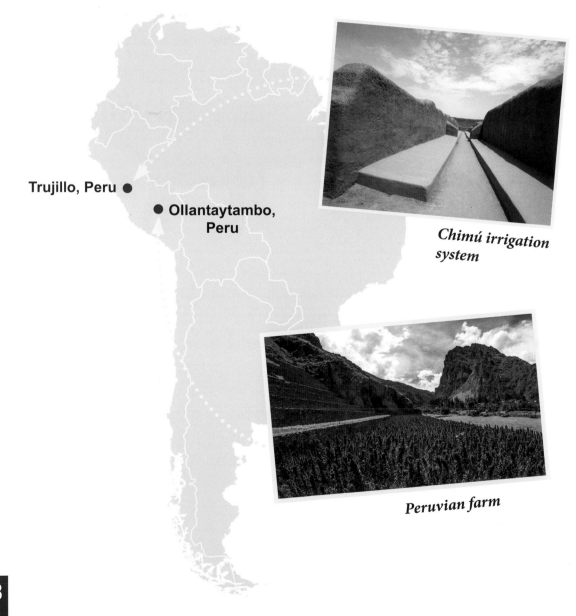

Trujillo, Peru ●

● Ollantaytambo, Peru

Chimú irrigation system

Peruvian farm

Later, the Incas, an ancient group of people in Peru, used step agriculture. They built **terraces** in the hillsides that looked like stairs. This created areas of flat land where farmers grew crops and kept animals.

This hill in Pisac in the country of Peru would have been too steep to use for farming without terraces.

Farming with the Past

Farmers in Peru have changed how they work. They started repairing and using irrigation systems originally made in ancient times. These systems use less electricity and are better for the environment than modern ones.

ON THE MOVE

Bridges are important in South America. Margaret D. Lowman, also called **Canopy** Meg, is a pioneer in treetop science. She studies things that live in the canopy, especially in very old trees. She invented canopy walkways that make exploring easier.

Canopy Meg has written several books about her experiences.

Walkways like this one help visitors see things in the canopy that they could not see from the ground.

The Capac Ñan, or the Great Road, also had suspension bridges woven from natural fibers. It was made by the Incas nearly 600 years ago. It stretched over 25,000 miles (40,000 kilometers) along the Western coast of South America. It was a very advanced road system. Ancient engineers built its dirt paths, stone roads, and stairways.

Some parts of the Great Road were carefully lined with stones.

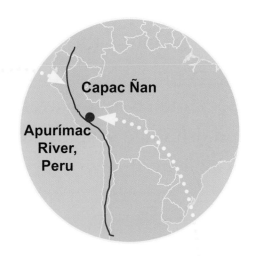

Yearly Ritual

Q'iswa Chaka is the last remaining suspension bridge from the time of the Incas. It crosses the Apurímac River. People who live nearby get together to repair the bridge once a year.

BUILDING FOR EARTHQUAKES

Inca inventors were skilled at building with stones. They built Machu Picchu, a huge stone city that still stands in Peru. Historians think it was built by Pachacuti Inca Yupanqui, the ninth ruler of the Inca. The people who helped build Machu Picchu used many layers under buildings and drainage systems that let rain flow away from them.

Machu Picchu,
Peru

Pachacuti Inca Yupanqui lived from 1418 to 1471 or 1472.

The remains of Machu Picchu are visited by tourists from around the world.

South America is one of the most earthquake-prone places on Earth. Buildings must be made so they will not get damaged when the ground shakes. Arturo Arias, an engineer from Chile, invented a way to measure movements in Earth's surface. His method is used to study the earthquake risk of an area. His method was used to make new building safety standards in the country of Chile.

Ancient architects also designed structures strong enough to resist earthquakes. Inca builders did not use mortar between the stones. Instead, they cut granite or limestone blocks to fit perfectly together. During an earthquake, the stones shift and then move back into place.

Police check a neighborhood after an earthquake in Santiago, Chile.

The stones in the ancient buildings in Machu Picchu bounce during an earthquake and then fall back into place.

Sliding Stones

The ancient building technique of cutting stones to fit perfectly together is called *ashlar*. Thanks to techniques like this, Machu Picchu and other very old buildings are still in good condition.

DISCOVERIES IN THE SKIES

Atacama
Desert, Chile

Clear, starry nights are common in the Atacama Desert.

In Chile, several **observatories** are used to view the incredible night sky. This part of South America has a clear sky, little rain, and almost no light pollution. It is easy to see stars and planets with telescopes such as those at the La Silla Observatory. Some scientists consider Chile the best place on Earth to look at space.

The La Silla Observatory is located at the edge of the Atacama Desert in Chile. It is about 7,874 feet (2,400 meters) above sea level and has clear skies almost year-round.

Astronomical Structures

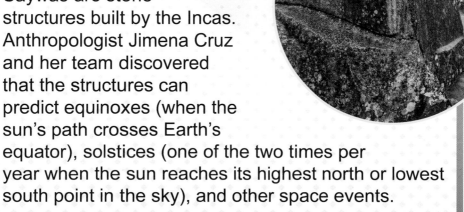

Saywas are stone structures built by the Incas. Anthropologist Jimena Cruz and her team discovered that the structures can predict equinoxes (when the sun's path crosses Earth's equator), solstices (one of the two times per year when the sun reaches its highest north or lowest south point in the sky), and other space events.

South America has many great minds in **astronomy**. In 1997, Chilean astronomer María Teresa Ruiz discovered two objects in space. They were too big to be planets and too small to be stars. They were named brown dwarfs. This pair of objects together is called Kelu-1. In 1997, she became the first woman to receive Chile's National Prize for Exact Sciences.

Adriana C. Ocampo grew up in Argentina with dreams of exploring planets. She helped discover the crater where an asteroid or comet slammed into Earth 65 million years ago.

That event may have resulted in the **extinction** of over half of all living species, including all of the dinosaurs.

María Teresa Ruiz used the La Silla telescope for some of her discoveries.

Adriana C. Ocampo started working in space research in high school.

This model shows what might have happened in prehistoric times. In this case, an object from space might have caused the crater that Adriana C. Ocampo discovered.

There are so many trees in the Amazon rainforest that they block out most of the sunlight that would reach the forest floor.

Serra do
Imeri, Brazil

Amazon
rainforest

DISCOVERING AND PROTECTING NATURE

The Amazon rainforest covers an area of 2,300,000 square miles (6,000,000 square kilometers) in South America. It is the world's largest tropical rainforest and has more than five million kinds of plants, animals, and insects. People find new living things all the time there!

In 2017, Miguel Trefaut Rodrigues and a team of scientists journeyed to Pico da Neblina, the highest mountain in the country of Brazil. The **Indigenous** Yanomami people gave them access to the protected area. Working together, they discovered nine new species of frogs, toads, birds, lizards, and plants.

Yanomami people live in the countries of Brazil and Venezuela. Some groups might live so far inside the rainforest that they have not been contacted by other people.

Pico da Neblina gets its name from the clouds that almost always cover it.

Scientists are hard at work trying to protect the Amazon and other natural areas in South America from burning, logging, and other harmful practices. Patricia Medici is a scientist from Brazil. She works to protect the largest land mammal in South America, the South American lowland tapir. She promotes **conservation** that protects the tapir and its habitat. She founded the Lowland Tapir Conservation Initiative to do this.

Patricia Medici has helped build a group of people around the world who want to help protect tapirs.

The Amazon River runs through the rainforest.

Tapirs are known as "the gardeners of the forest" because they eat fruit and spread the seeds in their droppings.

Modern Research Technology

Researchers use flying robots called drones to study the Amazon rainforest. The drones have sensors that can sense changes in plants. The researchers hope to understand how living things respond to changes in climate and the loss of trees.

NEW PLANTS, NEW HEARTS

Medical discoveries made in South America have improved the lives of people around the world. Plants have been used in medicines for a long time, especially by Indigenous peoples. South America is filled with many species that are not found anywhere else on Earth, especially in the Amazon rainforest. Some of the plants used by Indigenous peoples as medicine have been studied by scientists. They were shown to help treat diseases such as multiple sclerosis and Parkinson's disease.

Tena,
Ecuador

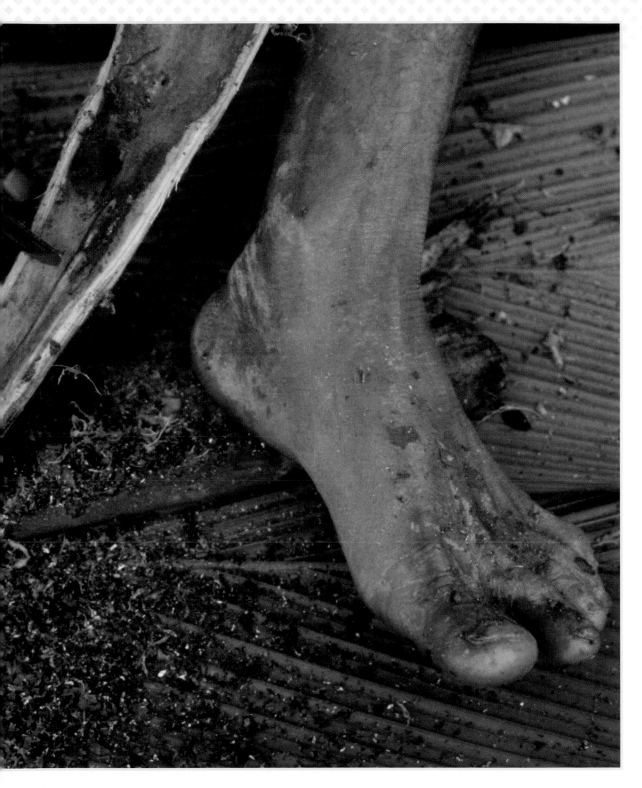

Indigenous peoples make paste, called curare, *from the bark of vines. Scientists have researched this paste for possible uses in medicine.*

The artificial heart that Domingo Liotta helped invent was made of cloth and plastic.

Domingo Liotta worked with several important doctors to improve medical science.

South American inventors have helped create new medical technology. Domingo Liotta, a surgeon from Argentina, changed how modern heart surgery is done and saved lives with the invention of the artificial heart. Julio C. Palmaz invented a type of medical balloon that can be inserted into the body. It is used to treat heart disease and other health problems.

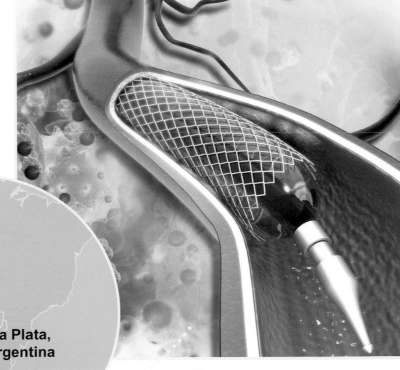

La Plata, Argentina

Córdoba, Argentina

Heart stent

STUNNING SOUTH AMERICA

South America is home to fascinating discoveries and inventions. From ancient buildings, to inventions by Indigenous peoples, to incredible new technology, South America has inspired many scientists, students, and researchers. How would your life be different without the great minds and finds of South America? The more you learn about South America, the more incredible things you will uncover.

Brazil

Chile

Argentina

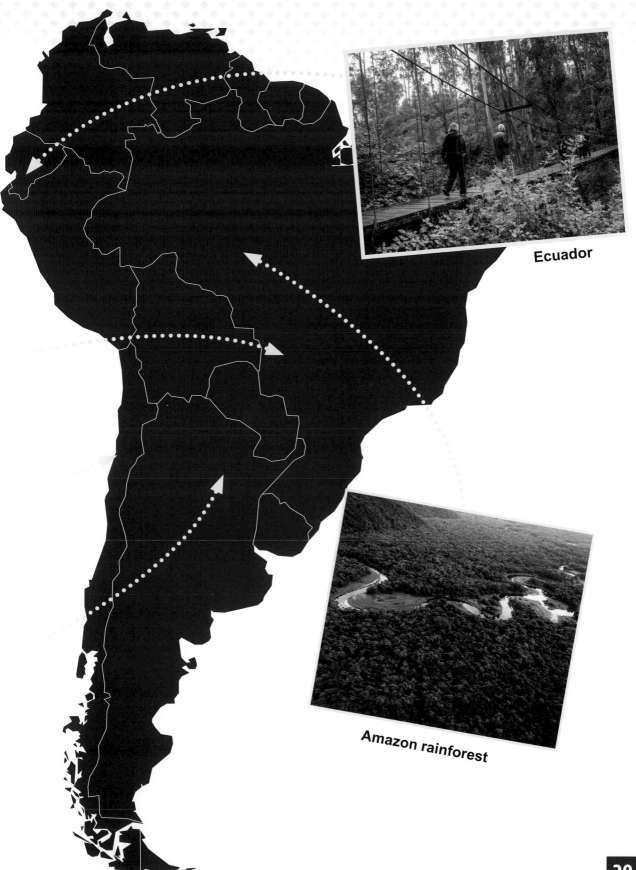

Ecuador

Amazon rainforest

Glossary

agriculture (AG-ri-kuhl-chur): the raising of crops and animals

aqueducts (AK-wuh-duhktz): large bridges built to carry water across a valley

astronomy (uh-STRAH-nuh-mee): the study of stars, planets, and space

canopy (KAN-uh-pee): the upper level of a rainforest

conservation (kahn-sur-VAY-shuhn): the protection of valuable things, especially forests and other things in nature

extinction (ik-STINGKT-shun): the process of living things dying until no more are found alive

Indigenous (in-DI-juh-nuhss): people living naturally or originally in a particular area

irrigation (ihr-uh-GAY-shuhn): supplying water to crops by artificial means

observatories (uhb-ZUR-vuh-tor-eez): special buildings that have telescopes and other machines for studying the stars and the weather

terraces (TER-is-ez): raised, flat platforms of land with sloping sides

Index

Amazon rainforest 20, 22–24

Andes mountains 6

Atacama Desert 6, 16, 17

Capac Ñan 11

earthquake(s) 14

Gallina, Pablo 7

Inca(s) 9, 11–14, 17

Machu Picchu 12–15

medicine(s) 24–27

Ruiz, María Teresa 18

Text-Dependent Questions

1. Why is Chile such a good place to see stars?

2. Why did the Incas build steps in hillsides?

3. What are some reasons that plants in the Amazon rainforest are important?

4. Why is anti-earthquake technology important in South America?

5. How can drones help protect rainforests?

Extension Activity

Plan a trip to South America. Decide what kind of places you would like to visit. Research several locations for your trip. Be sure to research the area's weather so you can plan what kind of clothes to bring.

About the Author

Robin Koontz is a freelance author and illustrator of books, educational blogs, and magazine articles for children and young adults. Her 2011 science title *Leaps and Creeps: How Animals Move to Survive* was an Animal Behavior Society Outstanding Children's Book Award Finalist. Robin lives with her husband in the Coast Range of western Oregon, where she especially enjoys observing the wildlife on her property. You can learn more on her blog: robinkoontz.wordpress.com.

www.rourkeeducationalmedia.com

PHOTO CREDITS: page 3: ©onceawitkin / iStockphoto.com; page 4: ©Puwadol Jaturawutthichai / Shutterstock.com; page 5: ©Sergio Hernán Gonzalez / iStockphoto.com (top); page 5: ©General/Photoshot / Newscom (bottom); page 5: ©Arunna / iStockphoto.com (binoculars); page 6: ©Alexandr Berdicevschi / iStockphoto.com (top); page 6: ©D'July / shutterstock.com (bottom); page 7: ©Slate Weasel / Wikimedia (top); page 7: ©Dornicke / Wikimedia (bottom); page 8: ©Watch The World / shutterstock.com (top); page 8: ©tbradford / iStockphoto.com (bottom); page 9: ©SL_Photography / iStockphoto.com; page 9: ©tirc83 / iStockphoto.com (bottom); page 10: ©Ascánder / Wikimedia (top); page 10: ©DavorLovincic / iStockphoto.com (bottom); page 11: ©Gfed / iStockphoto.com (top); page 11: ©Magnus Manske / Wikimedia (bottom); page 13: ©SL_Photography / iStockphoto.com; page 13: ©Zenobillis / iStockphoto.com (Inca Yupanqui); page 14: ©RJohn97 / iStockphoto.com; page 15: ©erlucho / shutterstock.com (top); page 15: ©CStephen / iStockphoto.com; page 16: ©Antonio Salaverry / shutterstock.com; page 17: ©abriendomundo / iStockphoto.com (top); page 17: ©Terri Butler Photography / shutterstock.com; page 18: ©Rec79 / Wikimedia; page 19: ©NASA; page 19: ©Elenarts / shutterstock.com (dinosaurs); page 20: ©FG Trade / iStockphoto.com; page 21: ©Cmacauley / Wikimedia; page 21: ©Naldo Arruda / Wikimedia (Pico da Neblina); page 22: ©afromusing / flickr (top); page 22: ©mantaphoto / iStockphoto.com; page 23: ©MikeLane45 / iStockphoto.com (tapir); page 23: ©Nerthuz / iStockphoto.com; page 25: ©John Wright / Eye Ubiquitous / Newscom (bottom); page 26: ©Karon Flage / flickr; page 27: ©Cliotta~commonswiki / Wikimedia (top); page 27: ©Mohammed Haneefa Nizamudeen / iStockphoto.com (bottom); background: ©DavidZydd / Pixabay

Edited by: Tracie Santos
Cover layout by: Kathy Walsh
Interior layout by: Book Buddy Media

Library of Congress PCN Data

Great Minds and Finds in South America / Robin Koontz
(Discoveries Around the World)
ISBN 978-1-73163-798-7 (hard cover)(alk. paper)
ISBN 978-1-73163-875-5 (soft cover)
ISBN 978-1-73163-952-3 (e-Book)
ISBN 978-1-73164-029-1 (ePub)
Library of Congress Control Number: 2020930269

Rourke Educational Media
Printed in the United States of America
01-1942011937